Space to BE:
Discovering a Life of Peace in 5 Steps

by Dawn M. McKinnis
Edited by Michael Jackson

ISBN: 978-0-578-42084-4

Dedication

I dedicate this book to the women who believe that there is MORE to their lives and feels lost figuring out a path forward.

I have been there.

I overcame it.

So can you!

This book was created with you in mind…God sees you and God has heard you. Let's journey back to our God-assigned Space of inner peace.

CONTENTS

ACKNOWLEDGEMENTS

God, I thank you for the grace and mercy extended to me throughout my journey in life. All that I have done and all that I desire to do is because of the love you have shown me when I felt lost, unsure, unqualified and unseen. I thank you and acknowledge you first because none of my gifts would have impact or power to heal without your spirit flowing through me.

To my husband, Michael and my son, Charles – the men in my life who love and support me through this transition and expansion of my life's purpose. Thank you for sharing me with the rest of the world! All of the challenges have been on purpose for a purpose! Love you both!

To my life coaches who have held my hand – both physically and virtually – as I explored the truth of who I am and why I am: Shanel Cooper-Sykes and Anna Debose-Hankins. You both have touched me in unique ways that I will never forget! I love you both dearly! Thank you!

To my circle…you know who you are! I love you all! We are being it! And this is just the beginning!

FOREWORD

In a world which seems increasing cold, confusing, and complex, it's easy to feel inescapably adrift in a sea of self-doubt and indecision. When I first read _Space to BE: 5 Steps to Create Space & Maintain Inner Peace in Your Daily Life,_ I was in just such a state. I was a newly widowed empty nester trying to find my personal and professional bearings and rediscover my purpose. But in this lost place, I uncovered this jewel of a book. Its universal observations, positive encouragement, and tools for self-examination were both a lighthouse and a lifeboat for me. A lighthouse, by which I could begin to reorient myself and rediscover my place and purpose. And a lifeboat to help me navigate towards the life I truly desire.

Space to Be is a thoughtfully intimate and inspiring blueprint for reevaluating our life's challenges and regaining control of its narrative. Peppered with personal anecdotes and challengingly interactive assignments, it's more than a simple 'self-help' book. Instead, it reads more like a conversation with a wise and encouraging friend. It's not a linear book one reads mindlessly through from beginning to end. Rather, it's designed for the reader's heart, head, and soul to chew on and digest its' wisdoms slowly. The reader should be prepared, after a chapter, a paragraph, or even a sentence to set it aside to contemplate, pray, meditate, and discuss the universal truths and personal applications found within its' pages. Then, pick it back up and begin the process again.

Michael Jackson, *Editor*

Michael Jackson is a political analyst/researcher and freelance writer/editor living in New York City.

HOW IT ALL BEGAN FOR ME

I have decided to share my story, though how much of its many twists and turns will remain in this book isn't my main concern right now. Instead, my focus is taking this first, crucially important step on my wellness journey. I'm sharing so others may understand with their minds and believe in their hearts that healing and freedom are possible. I have discovered that I am what's called a 'possibility pusher'! What does that mean for you? Well, it means this book is in your life at this moment not only to remind you of your possibilities, but also to assure you they're achievable if you *believe* them to be. If while reading you begin to think I've always had a courageous mindset and an unflinching belief in my own possibility, you would be mistaken.

For most of my life, I was repeatedly told what was **not** possible. That was always the implicit message from those around me, even when those exact words were not used. Many of these people may not have meant to be negative or discouraging. They may have been motivated by a need to protect me from failure or disappointment. I'm not sure how or where this fearful way of thinking originated among my family and friends, but I became determined to break free from it. Initially, I was comfortable maintaining a life of disbelieving all the dreams and aspirations so very clear in my mind's eye, while accepting dissatisfaction and unfulfillment as the norm. But no more. Today is a new day!

As a child, I had an active and vividly clear imagination. I would create elaborate scenes right before my eyes and engage in complete conversations which played out vividly in my mind. I was unaware at the time, but this skill for creating a richly imaginative world was being honed for the times when I'd need them most! Back then, envisioning idealized scenarios was a way for me to escape my, far from idealized, reality. I would always allow myself to wonder 'what if'. What if I lived with the wealthy people on 5th Avenue? What if I could fly like a bird over all these buildings and people? What if I could smell things from miles away like a wolf?

As you can see, I had quite an *active* imagination on me! What I know now is that these innocent childhood ponderings were actually quite deep examinations of the world and my place in it. I was really trying to understand the world from perspectives other than mine. Would I still be 'me' if I viewed the world as a wealthy person on 5th Avenue, from a soaring height, or could sense things from afar?

At some point along my journey, as is the case for most of us unfortunately, I allowed others to convince me that these imaginative ponderings and thoughtful questions were pointlessly wrong and should stop. I hid away my intuitive nature and inquisitive mind for many years. I accepted the destructive notion that it was irresponsible to 'hide away' in my imaginary land while life continued. But for brief moments every day, I would still sneak away inside myself and be transported to another time and place and explore what was possible. Maybe I would imagine an amazing life on a beautiful island or as a successful architect with my own firm. Until recently, I kept these escapes as my own little secret. I knew the outside world would never understand or appreciate the power of imagination. It's only since I've decided to openly and shamelessly *imagine* what is possible in my life, that I've truly begun to live.

For forty years, I'd lived a life of fear, doubt, disappointment, loss, and lack. Those feelings were my daily companions. When I was living according to those negative 'principles', I chose not to free those around me from being imprisoned by their fears and doubts as well. When I reflect on all those years of being blinded from my truth by fear and limitations, I can't help but wonder 'what if?' Although I lived through some painful moments over those years, they shaped me into the woman I am today. So, to wonder what my life would be without those scarring times would equal regret. I no longer regret **any** aspect of my journey no matter how painful! There is no place along your journey that is there by accident. There are no mistakes in life…only lessons. And it is because of my lessons that I'm writing this book.

***

Do you remember the movie, "Teen Wolf"? If you're my age, you'll remember the 1985 movie with Michael J. Fox. You might also know it as the

2011 MTV series with Tyler Posey. It was a story about a teenaged boy that turns into a werewolf during the full moon and all his challenges being both a teenager and a werewolf. I remember watching it and imagining, 'what if I were a werewolf?' What 9-year-old girl asks herself that kind of question? This kid! And I wouldn't just emotionlessly ask the question as a thought experiment. I would become a wolf...yeah, I did. I would walk around sniffing things, turning my neck like I believed a wolf man would. I would walk on all fours around the house and think, "how would a wolf respond to this?" At that time in my life, I would **never** share this 'daydream' with family or friends because they would have thought it was weird and even a little morbidly dark. I realize now that those were the important characteristics of empathy bubbling up in my personality. Empathy is defined as the ability to understand and share the feelings of another. So, it wasn't that I was being weird or demonic, but empathetic and even emotionally intelligent! Those so-called daydreams haven't stopped by the way. However, now I have a definite purpose for them and intentionally use my mind's imaginative creativity to create what I desire in my life. I'm writing this book to let you know you can do the same thing and to show you how. ***It is possible!***

I remember one day my life coach, Shanel Cooper-Sykes, asked me to do a life-changing assignment. She wanted to teach me to expand the limits of what I thought possible for my life by dreaming bigger. She encouraged me to write down a 'snapshot' of my life as I imagine it. It wasn't supposed to be based on my current reality, but rather on the power of my imagination and belief in my life's purpose. This exercise started out simply as a fun activity, but ***quickly*** blossomed into a way of ***living***…and this is how it started:

"I am so happy and grateful for the acceptance of my design proposal on a new multi-million dollar office building contract! Ever since becoming licensed, it has been my dream to land this one! This 10-year contract will allow me to bring prosperity and wellness into the lives of thousands of my employees. Upon my return from a much-needed month-long vacation to Matera, Italy, I will meet with my team to begin the design process. I also know my coaching clients will understand my need for a brief escape with my husband...who's been receiving ten photography contracts weekly and has never been happier! His team is

excellent and will easily handle all his affairs while we are away.

Oh! And join me in congratulating my son Charles on his promotion into NASA's Special Programs Machining Division as a Team Lead! His 4.0 GPA at the University of Maryland College Park, along with his innovative designs, paved the way for this opportunity. But before he starts this position, he is taking a cross-country trip to California in his Jeep Wrangler with a few of his friends to celebrate! Send him lots of love and ENERGY for the road! Life is simply amazing! God gets ALL the glory!"

***

This one exercise challenged me to expand my mental horizons. First, by creating what I desire in my mind. Then, by supporting and nurturing my goals with strong, positive feelings in order to manifest them in the physical world. This strategy of *'Go there before you go there'* changed my entire life. It allowed me to live in possibility and expose myself to its reality. Even now, I am overwhelmed with emotion when recalling the beautiful life I see through the eyes of my imagination. I am now a firm believer that our imagination is a gift from God to remind us of who we truly are. It reminds us to **see** and **believe,** despite what the reality of the world around us reflects at any given time. It was such a powerful exercise that I have now turned it into a daily activity. Through this daily ritual of affirmation and positive projection, I have shifted my heart and mind to believe my aspirational visions more than the sensory perceptions of my natural eyes.

Some may call this naïve or unrealistically hopeful, but each time I step into that realm of possibility, nothing else matters or compares!

There comes a time in your life's journey when you must make the intentional decision to believe in yourself over the expectations, opinions, and statements of anyone or anything else. To believe in your possibility over the unending phone calls from debt collectors. To believe in your possibility over voices from your past whispering stinging critiques of all your former mistakes. To believe in your possibility and stand firm in that belief when life shouts in your face *"This is NOT possible!"* That's when it is time to stand straight and tall and shout back at life with a resounding, *"It IS possible!"*

Do you trust yourself enough to believe in your possibility? Can you see a snapshot of your best life clearly in your mind? Clear enough to live an *entire* day as if it were your current reality? If that sounds like a challenging image, you have some limiting beliefs which need uprooting. Just like ugly weeds choking a bed of fragrantly beautiful roses. Those limits need to be replaced with the truth of who you truly are in *God's eyes*, not those of society, friends, or even family. When we allow limiting beliefs to veil our eyes, the life we were divinely created and designed to live becomes cloudy, fragmented, and out of reach. One of the most important tasks on our journey through life is removing these obstructions. Once removed, we are then free to explore the beautiful truth of ourselves which had always unknowingly been right there in front of us. To expose the '*you*' that has been waiting to be freed from the prison of fear we have created for ourselves. Living in complete freedom is the only way to experience a life of true and holistic wellness. Will you feel free immediately? Probably not. But, with intentional daily actions toward your goals, a life of freedom and possibility is within your grasp…you just have to believe it, *see* it, and take it.

Have you ever heard the saying 'fake it 'til you make it'? I must admit I cringe every time I hear someone say those words. I mean, when is it *ever* a good and sustainable idea to fake a part of your life? Though I understand what this phrase is attempting to convey, no one can achieve the life they want by faking. The only goal of 'faking it' is to attempt to convince others of something, while neglecting the only person that truly matters… *you*. Faking implies your actions and behaviors aren't truly who you are in that very moment. That you're disingenuously working to convince others you are someone else. Would you make a real lifelong commitment to something or someone that you don't believe is real? I know I wouldn't. Ultimately, faking it is corrosive to your true goals since the entire time you don't actually believe what you've put so much work into getting others to believe.

You must truly **believe** in the life you seek! Instead, I prefer the following catchphrase, "**Be** it before you **see** it!" Do you see the difference? 'Being' implies you are already the embodiment of a thing, rather than just performing a role. It is not something far off in the future you would like to happen. No, it is happening now, and you are enjoying the experience now. Everything in your life reflects what you are being, and it must flow from the inside of your soul out to the real world. Not vice versa. That is the **key** to living the full possibility of your life. Being who you know you are **now,** and then allowing reality to match that belief.

For as long as I can remember, I fantasized about being different people and things. I would imagine being a bird soaring high above the noise of life. I would walk around the house with my head high and almost glide from room to room. Then, there were times I'd imagine being a world-famous celebrity. Again, I would walk with my head high, smiling and walking on my tip toes (mostly because celebrities in my mind *always* wore high heels!) There were even times when I'd imagine being a mean person, someone hostile every moment of life. I would walk around angrily glaring at people and never smile. I was using my imagination to explore every aspect of the human experience and even the animal world (as best as a human possibly could). I discovered, when fully immersed in each role, my entire mindset and movements would emulate that person or creature. It was an amazing breakthrough and quite fun for me, but something great artistic performers have known for years. When you completely believe the vision in your mind's eye about who you are and what you deserve, your entire body will follow! You will walk differently.

You will talk differently. You will work differently. And you will love **very** differently.

Embodying your possibilities, before they are physically manifested in the natural world, is the best way to create and sustain the life of holistic wellness you desire. It must be an 'inside job', one that originates in your thinking and then permeates outward into your entire being. For years, I tried to convince myself I was worthy of a healthy body and loving soul. I prayed prayers suggested by well-meaning people. I ate foods I was told would be best for me, spoke affirmations some websites suggested might help in weight loss. I prayed more and researched further...**nothing** changed.

As I reflect on it now, my health was progressively becoming worse despite all my effort. It got to the point where I had to be admitted to the hospital. During all this **doing**, I was never actually **being** who I desired to become. Subconsciously, I didn't fully believe my prayers because I wasn't embodying the words once they'd been spoken. I didn't wholeheartedly believe my affirmations because I didn't connect them with the image of myself in the mirror. I was essentially dressing up a dead woman who had no idea she was dead. As grim as that may sound, it was 100% true. The day I realized this, I cried. I wept because I'd thought for so long the condition of my life was a sort of punishment. Therefore, I didn't deserve anything better. But once becoming aware of my life's possibilities and the power God had provided through my words and my *faith*, my entire life was renewed. It truly was an inside job!

Now, I know many people have become leery of the whole 'speak things into existence' philosophy. Far too often, it's been overly marketed as a gimmick by self-help gurus. But that should not discount the truth behind those words. We are creators, made in the image of God. The same God who **spoke** the world into existence, and so we do the same thing every time we open our mouths to speak. Are you intentional with your words? Or do you speak without thinking most days...not realizing the power within your words? Many of us are living lives we don't want because of thoughtlessly spoken words. Maybe these are words you have heard all your life and have become a habit, a part of how you see yourself. Maybe there are thoughts and beliefs you have subconsciously lived by, but never actually questioned. Whatever those words, thoughts, or beliefs are, they're manifesting in your life *right now*. So, what do you do about it?

As I began to take *intentional* actions in my daily life, I recognized that it's essential to follow a specific process to live a life of peace and experience more *good*. That is when the title for this book emerged, "Space to BE". I recognized that everything I was doing created an opportunity to truly BE who God designed me to be. That renewing my intentional thoughts, words, and actions could provide me the greatest opportunity for peace each day.

Does it always work perfectly? Of course not!

But it works! And I want to guide you through the 5 steps I take to create and maintain Space to BE in my daily life….

So, let's get started!

Step One:
Understand Your Needs

Clearly and fully understanding your needs is the first step in any path to self-discovery and true freedom. It is essential that you both identify, and plainly define those things you truly desire to have in your life. No vague goals like 'get in shape' or 'find my soulmate', but rather asking you what's at the core of your dreams and aspirations. Many of us are living undesirable lives because we honestly have no idea what we **actually** want in life. We slide in and out of roles and labels without giving a thought to where we are, where we're headed, or if we even want to go there. We just morph from being someone's child/sibling to a student to an employee, (maybe) to a spouse to a parent, to a boss. We continue existing for others, or for what we feel society expects from us, and never stop moving long enough to ask, "Wait, who am I *truly* and what do I need to BE to live as that person?" Does that sound familiar? Have you looked up and realized you've lived for over half of your life for *others*? I did…and it truly hurt. It hurt to realize that I'd never given myself permission to BE.

Before we go any further, I want to make something *very* clear… It is not an accident you are reading this book at this exact moment in your life. You have made the effort to invest your money, time and energy into purchasing, reading, contemplating, and implementing the message in this book. This means you've also made the conscious decision to understand who you are, and learn the steps required to grow and elevate your life. You have an abiding sense that you're *more* than you have become. It also means you're wise enough to understand that you'll need some assistance shedding the layers of 'stuff' between you and your God-created purpose. The mere fact you've decided to do this tells me, and should also tell you, a miracle of self-discovery and renewal is happening in your life right now!

However, now you've recognized the need for a change, you need to ask yourself, "a change *to* what, and *for* what?" What is it *really* that you need more of in life right now?

More Money?   More Time?   More Power?

More Influence?   More Love?   More Fun?

More Compassion?   More Faith?

Each one of us on this planet requires certain unique things to become who God made us to BE. However, most of us do not understand what those requirements are, or even fully realizes our true purpose. Additionally, it's not enough simply having a sense of your purpose on Earth, though this is an essential starting point. Each of us must identify what we require to achieve that purpose. We are so often oblivious to how the absence or presence of both these critical requirements impacts our lives and our happiness.

Have you ever wondered what's the true definition of the word 'need'? I did, so I decided to look it up! One thing you should know about me is that I've always had a *love* for words and their meanings! I have always loved discovering new words, their origins, and their actual definitions, as opposed to what people think they mean.

Need - to ***require*** something because it is ***essential*** or very important.

For a person to 'require' something indicates it's for a particular purpose, not just random or arbitrary. It must be specific and necessary for your life! What makes it necessary is that it is essential, central, and ***crucial*** to your identity and to your life's purpose. This exercise is the first step in creating a 'space to BE' in your daily life. By breaking down the words and their definitions, you can begin to sense the full magnitude of their role in your journey of self-discovery. It is paramount that you have a deep understanding of your ***needs!*** Let's move onto the word ***understand*** because it has a much deeper connotation than most people realize.

> **Understand** - to **_perceive_** the **_intended_** meaning of words, language or speaker; to infer something from information **_received_**.

Let's explore this definition...

For a person to **_perceive_** something is for them to *"become aware or conscious of it"*. I mentioned earlier how many of us are living obliviously unaware of our needs, or even why we require them in the first place. We often haven't become aware or conscious of these needs due mainly to our family upbringing and childhood environment. I'm sure you've heard people say things like, "I get nervous when everything's going right in my life", or, "I feel comfortable in dysfunction because that's all I know". And they are right! On a subconscious level, that's all they are aware of as a possibility for their lives. Can you relate to that?

Intended - Planned or meant.

This word's definition exudes a sense of *purpose* and purposefulness. When you use the word 'intend', you are declaring, "Hey, what I've said about my needs, I meant every single word of it!" But, when we haven't taken the time to discover our true needs, distracted by the demands of others, materialism, or society's expectations of us, we live a life adrift. Our life lacks both purpose and direction. And we can begin to feel hollow.

Received - To be given, presented with or paid something.

How do we receive something if we are closed? Can anyone be given something with closed hands, closed eyes, closed ears, or a closed mind? Of course not! You receive when you are open to new information or a new way of thinking. Then, you must be willing to absorb and integrate what's been given into your daily life. You receive only after the realization there is something you **need** and isn't already in my possession.

So, what does all this mean for you? Understanding your needs is **a process of becoming conscious and aware of a specific and necessary component/desire/truth/seed for your life with intention!** Please understand that this is a *process*. Going through the assignments in this book only once will *not* uncover your greatest need. It will start you on a journey, but you must be committed to this journey daily. Only through this deep commitment, along with actively changing your intentional actions, will you begin to *fully* understand what it is that you need.

I'm going to share a part of my journey with you who directly illustrate both the value of understanding your *true* needs, and how strong a resistance to change can manifest in one's life. Throughout my life, God has been trying to teach me powerful lessons which have often involved physical pain and discomfort. When I started wanting and believing a different narrative for my life, I saw the possibilities for a better, more purposeful way of living. As my mind and spirit began to walk towards this vision for myself, my body began to resist. Its resistance manifested in the form of painful physical symptoms.

Suddenly, one evening after drinking a glass of grape juice, I began to have an allergic reaction – similar to the kind I've had before after drinking alcoholic beverages. For an entire week, simply breathing was extremely difficult for me. Obviously quite concerned, I went to an urgent care facility and was given an inhaler to help me breathe. I hadn't used an inhaler since childhood! Ironically, just a few days before, I'd decided once again to commit to exercising regularly and formed a 21 Day Accountability Group with some friends. I became so discouraged because it seemed like each time I made a conscious decision to step out on my belief and faith, an obstacle would appear in my way. I learned throughout that ordeal not to push myself from a place of anger or fear, but instead trust myself through the process and continue to love my body. Two weeks later, my breathing returned to normal, but I began to have an irregular heartbeat, or cardiac arrhythmia, due to stress. As I drove to the Emergency Room, I began to ask God, "What is happening to me?!" It seemed like either I'm not as healthy as I thought, or there is something I need in my life to thrive that I'm just not getting. It turned out, it was the latter.

After receiving electrical stimulation at the hospital to shock my heartbeat back into rhythm, I began receiving several profound revelations about who I am and who I am not. Unfortunately, too often it takes a brush with death or a family trauma for us to stop long enough and quiet our mind to hear God's still, small, voice. As I laid in the Emergency Room watching the medical staff place the electrical pads on my chest, I began to clearly see what had been sitting just below the surface of the beliefs and actions of my daily life. I'd caused a physical manifestation of my divided existence by my way of thinking. I sat there, watching my I.V. fill with anesthesia, realizing that somehow my way of thinking and being had broken my own heart. My outlook on life, and my place in it, had caused a schism between my spiritual, mental, and physical self.

Everything I thought I understood about the mind-body connection was expanded and illuminated to me during this experience. I gained a greater understanding and a deeper, more profound appreciation for the amazing masterpiece and divine blessing that's the human body. In those moments of distress, God revealed to me that I'd been living with a divided heart towards Him and my true self. I learned it is possible to make yourself sick with the power of your thoughts and your worldview. In my specific case, I learned it is possible to break one's own heart. When we send contradictory signals, of both *Fear* and *Faith*, our heart can lose rhythm and bring pain and sickness to our entire body. This is true for all aspects of our physical health, not just our hearts. When we walk out of step with our calling and are disjointed from our purpose, our physical health suffers from a form of spiritual arrhythmia. Sometimes we may believe we're walking through our lives in full faith, but our subconscious mind doesn't truly believe. It is corrupted by doubts and negative self-talk that undermine our faith.

The space between the conscious and subconscious can sometimes be so vast that your body, in my case my heart, negatively responds and manifests the gap as 'dis ease' or disease. My traumatic medical incident made me realize I hadn't been kind to myself. In all of us, there is a constant, delicate dance between our conscious and professed beliefs on the one hand, and our subconscious fears, anxieties, and insecurities on the other. This dance can very quickly turn into a self-destructively painful fight if we don't monitor, confront, and actively rebut negative self-talk in our minds. I had a decision to make at that moment. Would I continue forward with the limiting thoughts and beliefs that had allowed this medical emergency to unfold? Or should I start tilling the soil of my mind, uproot these negative weeds, and begin to cultivate the spiritual garden of my happiness and inner peace?

Through these events and others, I've learned the purpose and power of our belief systems, our inner voices, and our thoughts. I have explored, interrogated, and challenged the fundamental beliefs which govern the way I live my life and experience the world around me. It has been, and continues to be, a fascinatingly fulfilling, though sometimes painful, journey. One filled with many 'ah-ha' moments of spiritually uplifting self-revelation. However, there have also been plenty of 'oh-no' moments where I realized past missteps of entrenched negativity and self-sabotage as well. But that is the beauty of this journey of self-discovery and improvement on which you have embarked. It is the beauty of life itself. Every moment is a necessary thread in the tapestry of our life. It is all necessary!

The week that followed my 'broken-heart' session taught me to take responsibility for the seeds of negativity planted in my mind which were no longer serving me well. Blaming someone else or some other circumstance outside of my own thinking will never correct the unfulfilled condition of my life. Once I acknowledged the role others played in my inner turmoil and unhappiness, I decided to forgive them, release them to God, and move forward in the hard work of healing my inner landscape and planting new seeds of positivity.

Mindset renewal can be very much like caring for a real garden. When I'm assessing the condition of the real-life garden in the backyard of my home, I obviously notice the beautiful flowers, lush bushes, and majestic trees. But, I must also notice the choking weeds which may also have grown as strong and tall as the trees in my garden. These weeds may have been seeded by birds, rodents, insects, or even the wind without my knowledge. They may be parasitically wrapped around the flowers, plants, and trees, while slowly sucking the life out of the beautiful flora and fauna of my garden. Regardless of their origin, I have a decision to make:

I can spend my time wondering who planted these hideous, unsightly weeds and ruminating on how I could've neglectfully let them grow so long unnoticed.

OR

I can put on my gloves and begin uprooting.

Let's walk through each option and see where it takes us.

Option 1: *Who* Did This?!

I frustratingly stand at the edge of my deck, looking at all the weeds slowly choking my beautiful garden and begin having a fuming tantrum! "Who would do this?" "Why *my* garden?" "This will take forever to correct!" I go back inside the house trying to uncover *when* this happened and **who** had contact with my garden. Fruitlessly relitigating the past to find blame for something which is already occurring and pointlessly struggling to find clues on how this could have happened.

Option 2: Let's Get to Work!

I stand at the edge of my deck, looking at all the weeds slowly choking my beautiful garden and, instead of seeing what is, begin to imagine what is possible. "Ok, now this looks like a complete mess, but I know with a little planning and focus, I can turn it around! Harvest is coming and I plan on being ready to receive it! What should I focus on first?

Meditate on this Question:

Do you want to live the same year twice?

Let that sink in for a minute. When I first considered this question, the implication of being stuck in the same mental space, like a bizarre 'Ground Hog Day' or scary Twilight Zone episode, it struck a fearful cord, deep in my soul. My answer was a resounding NO!! How about you? Did the prospect of repeating each day for a whole year hit you the way it did me when I first heard it? Honestly, you must ask yourself whether you want to remain in the same mental space you are currently in. Or will you *allow* yourself to grow and flourish into the purposeful life God intended for you? It's time to do the *work* friends!

Assignment #1:

There's something within your mind which may be not only blocking you from achieving your greatest desire, but also stopping you from permanently possessing your greatest need. I would like you to dig deep, remain authentically truthful to yourself, and answer this question:

1. What is the source of my fear of going for my heart's desire?

Assignment #2:

Take some quiet time during your day to answer these questions, with **complete** honesty and authenticity, in order to fully understand your needs:

1. What situations/ attitudes/environments irritate me?
2. What situations/attitudes/environments anger me?
3. What situations/attitudes/environments bring me peace without trying?
4. What situations/attitudes/environments bring a smile to my face?

Resource Suggestion: *To assist you in these assignments, consider using the Just BE Bundle found at* *www.atmospheresofwellness.com/shop*

Step Two:
Shift Your Perspective & Perception

I have been in the architecture and construction industry for over 18 years and love what I do. However, I must admit that my favorite part of the design process isn't the finished product, or the accolades that sometimes come with it. My absolute favorite part of the whole process occurs at the very first client meeting. That's when we ask the client, "What do you need?" Then they share their desires for the project. It's at that point we use our experience and expertise to gently tell them, "No, that is actually not what you really need. Let's help you figure this out." This is exactly what I'm saying right now about your process of self-discovery while reading and digesting this book's message.

I'm sure after completing the assignments within Step One, you're feeling one of two emotions: **Confidence** or **Confusion**. Confident you've identified the roots of your needs, while feeling pumped to go for it! However, you might instead feel confused, overwhelmed because you've no idea what steps to take next in order to fully experience the better life you desire. To both these reactions, I say BREATHE!! Discovering new territory can be emotional and overwhelming if you forget your 'why'. You remember your 'why', right? Your purpose for saying yes to reading this book and doing the hard work of true self-discovery. Your 'why' is the burning desire to establish space to BE and experience *peace* in your daily life. So, let's take what we have discovered about ourselves and *shift.*

Step two in this process is foundational to the successful renewing of your mind and freeing of your spirit. We will take what we've learned already about the confining nature of our current mindset and *shift* it in both perspective and perception. But first, let's head over to the dictionary! (You should know this part by now!)

Shift - to put something ASIDE and REPLACE it with another; change or exchange

Perspective - the STATE of one's ideas, the facts known to one, etc. in having a meaningful interrelationship; a mental view or prospect. Perspective is the HOW of your thinking...how you see life.

State - a particular condition of mind or feeling.

Perception - the act or faculty of perceiving or apprehending by means of the senses or of the mind; cognition. (*In psychology*) A single unified awareness derived from sensory processes while a stimulus is present.

Put simply, perception is the *'what'* you receive from thinking about what you believe about life. For example, what if my husband and I were walking down the street one day and came across a couple arguing. The man wasn't saying anything and was looking away into space, while the woman was yelling and moving her arms around angrily. When we passed them, I turned to my husband and said, "He's a jerk!" My husband, just as emphatically said, "No, she's a jerk!" My *perception* was that the man was at fault.

I figured he was at fault given that he'd not only had no rebuttal to her yelling, but also showed a lack of concern for her feelings by not even looking at her. However, my husband's *perception* was the woman was being demeaning and verbally abusive. He pointed to the fact that she was yelling at him in front of everyone on the street. Meanwhile, the man was quietly looking away in an effort to remain calm in the face of her abuse. Our interpretations of who 'the jerk' was in that situation were informed not by knowing the content of the confrontation, but by our differing *perspectives* as a man and a woman.

So, considering these definitions and examples, how do we **shift** (*change the direction of a thing*) our **perspective** (*attitude about a thing*) and our **perception** (*our awareness of this attitude*)? How do we change the direction of our attitudes about things in our lives, while also changing our awareness of those things? To help answer these questions, I want to share another part of my wellness journey with you...

On September 10, 2015, I started my day like every other day by going to my job as usual. However, by the end of the day, I was looking out of the hospital window, recovering after receiving an emergency blood transfusion, and asking myself, "How did I get here?" That's all I kept thinking the entire day. How did I go from someone committed to working out daily and changing her eating habits to a hospital bed with an I.V. in my arm? How could this happen to someone who'd felt perfectly fine just 24 hours before? I was confused and asking God for answers. Although at the time I believed I was ready for the answers, I now know I truly wasn't in the frame of mind to receive it.

A week later, I was back in the hospital suffering from a racing heartbeat and dizziness. The doctors diagnosed me with pulmonary emboli, or blockages caused by blood clots, in both of my lungs. Again, I sat there wondering, "How?" This life-threatening medical emergency started me on a journey of self-discovery and a burning desire to be well. I knew that this was not the life I wanted, but at the time, wasn't emotionally or spiritually equipped with the tools to change it. All I had were inspirational words with no clear direction or purposeful intention. Most of you can relate to this situation.

Six months after that diagnosis, I was taken off of blood thinners and trying to prepare myself for a hysterectomy. Yes, it seemed as though my body was breaking down and failing month by month, and I was at a complete loss to stop it. "How did I get here?" was my constant refrain. In April 2016, I had the surgery and began a period of social isolation and silence. I had no other choice while recovering from the procedure but to be still and listen to God speak to me in his small, still voice. During this time, I discovered I was amazing at loving and caring for everyone else, but had absolutely no clue how to do the same for myself. I knew that if I continued in that same pattern, my family wouldn't have me around much longer. It was a jarring realization, but what was even scarier at that time was I had **no idea** how to change. I'd read the books, gone to therapy, prayed, journaled... And yet, there I was, still hurting both physically and emotionally.

On August 26, 2016, I turned 40 years old. As I thought over the first 40 years of my life, I asked myself, "How have I impacted the world? Have I lived a life that I can be proud of?" The answers which came to mind saddened me. So I decided right then and there that my next 40 years would not be more of the same. I began intensely seeking someone who could walk with me through this season of emotional release, self-exploration, and spiritual elevation. Fortunately, I connected with a life coach who helped me through a quite intense and sometimes unpleasant journey of exposure, uprooting, and replanting. Even before we began, I knew I'd never be the same and that a new possibility for my life was being uncovered. Through daily intentional actions, I better understood that the life I'd lived was a result of consistent thoughts and actions. She helped me realize that at any moment, I'd had the power within me to shift the trajectory of my life but just had chosen not to. The thing that helped me process this disheartening information was one statement… *'You didn't know.'* When I finally fully realized our lives unfold in undesirable ways because we don't know any better, it gave me hope. It showed me I had more power over my life's outcomes than previously realized. I started to question what was truly possible for my life – in relationships, health, wealth and career. It was at that point I had my first major 'ah-ha' moment. *All* my dreams are possible! For example, I'd grown up believing the business world wasn't for me because of my empathetic and non-aggressive nature. At that moment, I had an epiphany. Not only was it untrue that I couldn't be a successful businesswoman, but those very attributes of empathy and kindness were God's gift to me and were meant to be used to help others.

What I want you to fully understand is that *change is possible*! You may be thinking, "Well Dawn, it's great you changed your way of thinking after going through all those struggles, but you don't know my story! I can't change now." Or maybe you think, "It can't be that simple. Just make a decision to change how you think? C'mon!" But it is. However, just because it's a simple concept doesn't mean it will be quick or easy to integrate into your life. It's a conscious and deliberate choice to change the way you think about a thing each and every time you encounter it. You will hear me repeat a phrase over and over and over again in this book. ***Daily Intentional Actions.*** I will explain it in detail later, but for now, just understand that you ***must*** decide ***every day*** to shift your perspective and perception.

Renewing your mind takes two distinct steps – excavation and implementation. The first step, excavation, is a very delicate and intricate step. It will require you to dig deep into your subconscious mind, pull out your underlying belief systems, and examine each one with the intensity of a pure, white flood light. Have you ever been to a construction site during excavation?

It looks chaotic, busy, messy and fruitless. You can often wonder, "There is *nothing* happening right now! I see no progress!" And many times, during this spiritual excavation step, that's exactly how you may feel. You will be tempted by this seeming lack of progress to quit. ***Don't!***

During the second step, implementation, you begin to plant, build and create. By this point in the process, you've removed those things which no longer serve your purpose and are therefore prepared to create the life you truly desire. Using the same construction site analogy, you already will have the proverbial ground leveled and all the tools and resources ready to pour the foundation – cement truck, cement forms in place and all the workers needed for the task. We will discuss these "tools and resources" later in the book.

Assignment:

1. Write down some of your belief systems. Describe everything you can think of, from the small beliefs to the big ones.

2. Write down the name of the person(s)/experience(s) which led you to that belief. If you don't know who, write 'unknown".

3. FORGIVE! Yes, forgive them.

When I speak of these people, I'm not referring to those who've intentionally said mean and hurtful things in your life. The words which do the most damage in our lives are often from well-intentioned people whose opinions we respect. The loving Aunt who says your hair needs to be straightened because it's 'bad hair'. The friend who comments on recent weight gain or discourages you from starting a business or pursuing a dream. They had no idea of the consequences of their words to you. They never took the kind of time you are investing right now to understand the power of their words to impact your life. If they truly knew better, then they would do better. See them as a child attempting to fit into the shoes of a full-grown adult. That is basically what it equates to – Your parents, siblings, co-workers, and friends were given the power to create with their words, but most of them have no idea the magnitude of the power within them. But now, you do! And you can change that impact by releasing them today.

When I refer to experiences, I'm alluding to the beliefs we develop to cope with or explain of a specific circumstance or event. Sometimes we come to our beliefs in an effort to prevent a hurtful experience from reoccurring, or to rationalize a negative event. For example, you might come to believe you're not good at Math because you struggled in a particular class in school, or that you shouldn't travel by plane because you witnessed a plane crash. Sometimes we take the wrong lesson from an event in life which negatively affects us as we hold it throughout our life. Someone may hold a belief all men are abusive after being in an abusive relationship, or money is the key to happiness after growing up poor and unhappy. Again, forgive. In this case, forgive yourself. Realize you didn't know the long-term impact these beliefs would have on your life. You were trying the best you knew how to make sense of your circumstances and protect yourself. You now know better, so you can do better.

Step Three:
Elevate Your Knowledge

Over the past two chapters, I've described some of the intense emotions and revelations I've experienced. I can assure you, if you are still reading and doing the daily work, the life of peace you desire is right in front of you. Just waiting for you to receive it! Keep going! In this chapter, I'll be describing what I like to call the '*pivot point*'. What's a pivot point? As I began my journey of maintaining wellness and daily peace, I realized my perspectives on life and belief systems were critically determining factors in shifting and shaping my life. They impact whether I experience fear each day or peace. Becoming aware of triggers of my daily emotions and feelings has empowered me to consciously choose my responses to everyday situations.

PIVOT POINT - the center point of any rotational system; (economics) a time when a market price trend changes direction (technical analysis); a person or thing on which something depends; the central crucial factor. A dramatic change in policy, position or strategy.

All of us have experienced moments in our lives which we consider 'Pivot Points', either at the time they occurred or in retrospect. Jot down a few which immediately come to your mind. For example, having a baby, getting married, first job, first home, college graduation, etc. These are the obvious ones in our lives which are easy to see coming, and even easier to recognize once they have passed. However, many times, there are pivot points in our lives which are only recognized as being pivotal once some time has transpired. For example, a passing conversation with a friend which inspires you to change professions, or a chance encounter with a stranger that leads to a lifelong friendship. I'd like to think reading this book, and the revelations it inspires, will be another pivot point in your life. Through this book, God is asking you to completely stop moving in one direction and go in a different, more fulfilling one.

Let's think about this more deeply for a moment. Have you ever looked at an actual pivot point in the physical world? Like a door hinge, an athlete pivoting while playing a sport, a piece of equipment that pivots, or just noticed yourself pivoting while walking. Right now, I want you to visualize these pivot points in your mind. Get up and walk for five steps, then turn and *pivot* towards a different direction. You'll notice immediately that pivoting takes **energy** to do successfully. It takes **strength**. To pivot, you also must first have directional intentionality. Even before moving, you must first have decided your current direction needs to change, and then determine a better direction.

I want you to know this is what you're doing right now. You are pivoting your life away from old ways of thinking and being. You're turning towards a **greater and better** you! To continue on this new journey of thinking, speaking, and being, it's essential you also **elevate** your **knowledge**.

ELEVATE - Raise or lift something *up* to a higher position.

KNOWLEDGE - facts, information, and skills acquired by a person through experience or education; the theoretical or practical understanding of a subject; awareness or familiarity gained by experience of a fact or situation.

Now it's time to take what you *think* you know about yourself and your purpose on earth and lift them *higher.* High enough to connect with what God *knows* about you and *wants* from you. Through reading these exercises, and doing the hard work of introspection, you have begun to uncover your underlying belief systems. Those beliefs, both known and unknown, are operating every day in your life and creating your reality. Though you may be surprised, or even embarrassed, by what you've discovered so far, understand you do have the power and knowledge to change these belief systems. To sculpt the beautiful work of art God always intended you to be.

Assignment:

Create some 'Renewed Belief Statements'.

This exercise is meant to harness the power of your beliefs, visualizations, and self-talk (BVS). To transform these BVSs which once harmed, limited, and hindered you by:

1. Using them to **elevate** your life to a higher dimension, more in tune with God's purpose for you

2. Using the creative and infinite power of **your words** to craft a life which aligns up with your deepest burning desires, goals, and aspirations.

For example, shift from saying, "I've always been afraid of starting a business" to "It's possible for me to create and build a successful business!"

Let's discuss for a moment those two powerful tools: your words and desires. The Bible, along with many other religious texts, tells us God created us in His image. However, have you ever stopped to really grasp what that means? One day, my life coach described this concept in a way which was so incredibly vivid to me. I began to fully comprehend what this statement truly means. She told me to think of all the oceans of the Earth. To imagine their enormity, movement, composition, texture, abundance, and power. Water is water is water, right? Now imagine going to the beach, taking a cup out, and filling the cup with ocean water. Is the water that's now in the cup fundamentally any different from the water in the ocean you just scooped out? No, of course it's not. It is the same ocean in a smaller container.

Same composition, abundance, and power just now in a vessel.

That is who *you,* and who all of us, *really* are! We are a piece of the Divine, a unique expression of the substance of God, and the image of our Creator. This carries quite a lot of power. Unfortunately, we often ignore this power altogether, waste it striving for fleeting material gain, give it away by chasing the validation of others, or use to erode our self-worth through negative self-talk. We all have been given the authority and ability to *speak* into existence the life of peace and prosperity we desire. What does that life look like for you? Exploring the answer to that question is your homework assignment. No one, but Spirit has that answer for you. God knows exactly the right answer for each of us. However, only you can create both the quiet stillness to hear it, and the space in your life to receive it.

Step Four:
Design Your Atmosphere

In this lesson, we're focusing on designing our outer atmosphere. It's a short lesson in order for you to be able to get started doing the previous three chapter's homework as soon as possible. It's my own personal belief that everyone should have a space in or around their home just to BE. This means a safe place where each person can temporarily set aside the roles and responsibilities they perform for others throughout the day and attend to themselves. A space where you can take off the hat of mother/father, brother/sister, spouse/significant other, or boss/worker and just be you. Where you can pray, dream, meditate and visualize the life you desire. Where every day you can meet and speak with God to set the right tone for your day. When my life coach shared the power and importance of creating and maintaining a physical space in your life to pray, meditate and visualize, I'd no idea just how radically it would change my life. Initially, it was a fun shopping exercise to create a little cute area to sit and read. But then I decided to probe deeper.

In the Christian Bible's Old Testament and the Jewish Talmud, there was a special space within the Tabernacle where only the High Priest could go and communicate with God on behalf of the people of Israel. In Latin, it was called the Sanctum Sanctorum or The Most Holy Place – The Inner Room. And it's in this space that the priest would sacrifice to God on behalf of the people. It was a 'sacred space'. The word 'sacred' is defined as being set aside for God's purposes.

Upon understanding this concept, I made the connection between having a "cute area to sit and read" and my life requiring a sacred space which reflects my importance in God's eyes. I knew at that moment that *everyone* needed to have this type of space as well. Being trained and experienced in the architecture and design industry for nearly 20 years, I understand the power of a well-designed atmosphere on the wellbeing of those within the space. Right now, let's discuss the word "atmosphere" and its importance.

ATMOSPHERE - a surrounding influence or environment. *(In Art)* The pervading tone or mood

Our physical environment plays a powerful, and often unappreciated, role in the inner world of our mind and spirit. The physical space surrounding us impacts our thoughts, beliefs, self-image, our physical health, and even our outlook of the future. Ever notice how you can enter certain places like a park, a place of worship, or a spa and immediately relax? Now, how about being in a hospital emergency room, a courtroom, or a busy train station? Your mood almost subconsciously begins to slow down or speed up in response to these different surroundings. You might feel your tension or self-confidence increase or decrease. Similarly, you may even have a certain friend or relative whose very presence makes you feel more or less encouraged about your life. Your environment matters!

Today, I want you to take conscious steps to design, construct, and maintain an atmosphere in which you can be your *best* self. Rather than simply reacting to whatever atmosphere is thrust upon you. So far, we've been focusing on the crucial inner work of shifting our thinking and beliefs *(inner atmosphere)*. Now, it's time to connect these two interrelated components of our life. *(inner & outer atmosphere)*

Many times, if we pay attention, we can glimpse what's happening with a person by observing their physical environment. Do they have a messy car? Is their desk filled with random papers out of place? Are their closets cluttered with items they no longer use or need? Are they groomed on a regular basis? All these things are external ***indicators*** of a life in inner conflict and dis-ease.

It's possible for everyone to live a life of wholeness, healing, and abundance. And I'm not just talking about money or material possessions when I say abundance. Abundance relates to health, wealth, relationships and work! I truly believe that this is our birthright as beings created in God's image. Now, you must understand most people are not ***aware*** of this disconnection in their lives. Often, they feel they're just fine.

Unfortunately, ignorance is bliss for most of us. But there is a *grander* life available to us all, and a more *abundant* life at that! We can't judge them for what they don't know. But now that you have been made aware of these truths, you can adjust your atmosphere accordingly.

When I created my own sacred wellness space, I realized I needed a place to keep certain items or tools that were essential to me each day. That is where my 'wellness toolkit' came into play. I created it to remind me each day to step into my space and *love* myself. This is why I usually place the word *'Love'* on the top of each Toolkit. I will go into more detail about this in the next step. For now, get started on the homework and have fun!!

Assignment:

1. First, pray and/or meditate for Divine direction for the proper location of your sacred space within or around your home.

2. Once you have this location selected, clean it out completely and speak an intention for it. For example, "This area is sacred – set aside for God's purposes. Let it be so."

3. Shop for your space! Select textures, images, smells, and other items which elevate your beliefs and encourage your spirit! Think about each of your five senses and find something that soothes and re-centers each one of them.

4. Take a before and after picture. You will be amazed how much this shift in your atmosphere will change your environment! You will also have an example of how your intentional action has impacted your sense of peace.

Step Five:
Execute Your Daily, Intentional Actions

I have to admit, this is one of my favorite steps in this process. When deciding to change the way I viewed my life and take back control for my responses, I knew I'd needed a strategy to execute my desires. My life coach had taught me to create daily rituals and integrate them into every aspect of my life. However, I decided to implement rituals and activities to perform morning, noon and bedtime. I knew the serious amount of dismantling required in my life, so only once a day was simply not enough!

Now we're going to dive into establishing daily rituals which will increase your energy, elevate your thoughts, and create a space of peace which can only be disrupted *if you* allow it to be. *But first*, let's define this word *Ritual*. There were ten definitions before this one, but I didn't want to confuse our purposes of the word with it's' more common religious context.

> **RITUAL** - a prescribed code of behavior regulating social conduct, as that exemplified by the raising of one's hat or the shaking of hands in greeting. *(of an action)* arising from convention or habit.

This definition is best suited for our purpose given it's not necessarily related to a specific religious tradition. More so, it denotes the discipline and intention of actions performed daily. These actions are crucial for creating and maintaining peace in your life. The most essential component of these daily rituals is simply this – *Repetition, Repetition, Repetition!* We all know anything done repeatedly remains within your mind. This is the reason athletes practice incessantly, why kids can remember all the words to their favorite songs, and why advertisers pay hundreds of millions of dollars to get their products repeatedly in front of your eyes. Just reflect on all the negative words, events, and images which have been stuck with you until this book shined a light on them. They stuck because you heard, saw, and experienced them in your mind's eye over and over and over and over again. Now, we are simply resetting and replacing new habits, words, and actions into your life. These will create energy, power, passion, and abundance. Doesn't that just bring a smile to your face!

So, let me share some Daily Intentional Actions or D.I.A.s with you. D.I.A. is not only my acronym for these positive rituals, but it's also the word for *'day'* in Spanish. A perfect reminder to do this *daily*, right? I love it!

Here are ten daily rituals I use to create and maintain *Space to Be*:

One: Surrender

When I hear my alarm in the morning, I thank God for a new day and go straight to the place in my home which I've designated as my sacred wellness space. I get on my knees in the posture of surrender – head to the floor. It's at this point that I present God all of me. Every aspect of my life; family, health, wealth, career, business, relationships. I ask Him to take them out of my hands and purify them according to His will and plan for me.

Two: Gratitude

Next, I thank God for all He's given me. This is not just a happy list of gifts! No, this includes the struggles, hard lessons, pain, and the discomfort too. Every aspect of my life is *on purpose* for a *purpose*, so I thank Him for them.

Three: Prayer

There's so much which can be said on the topic of prayer. As I've been learning more about it, I've realized much of the way I'd thought about prayer has hindered the physical manifestation of my prayers. Asking for healing in my body yet believing subconsciously I deserve to be sick and punished for some assumed failure on my part. This kind of thinking will hinder your desire for healing immediately. You keep asking because you are not seeing any changes…and you never will. So, I'll say this, pray for a thing *once*. Then, thank

God for His provision of the object of the prayer according to *His* will *daily*.

Four: Music

Music has a way of healing a broken heart and energizing a weary body. Create a playlist on your smart device *specifically* for your daily rituals. Pick songs which energize, inspire, relax, or focus you depending on the time of the ritual's placement in your day. I've a morning playlist which always gets me going and keeps my energy and *positivity* high!

Five: Listening

In addition to music, I listen to motivational videos, audios, and podcasts every morning for at least 15 minutes a day. Typically, I listen to someone who inspires me, like Les Brown or Tony Robbins. I also listen to motivational audiobooks which are usually one to two hours in length. Don't break the bank though. You can find many of these inspirational speakers, motivational audiobooks, and podcasts for free on online sites like YouTube and even at your local library.

Six: Meditation

Please don't freak out about the word meditation. Meditation is simply holding a thought in your mind for an extended period of time. You can also think of it like the listening section above. However, during meditation, you're listening and observing your subconscious thoughts while focusing your mind. Chanting and swaying are not required! (You are more than welcome to if you desire!) Some meditation is simply sitting still and quiet, while others meditate with formalized ways of sitting or saying specific words or phrases. For me, meditation involves holding the word *peace* or *love* in my mind, repeating it over and over, and breathing calmly and deeply.

Seven: Repetitive Writing

I have a notebook in which every day I write down my affirmations, belief statements, or dreams. Whatever I'm believing for or focusing my mind on, I write it over and over and over again. Why? *Repetition* creates new habits and pathways within the brain which alter your physical world by changing the way you think! The actual practice of taking pen to paper and writing repetitively is not only soothing, but also a powerful transformational tool in mindset renewal.

Eight: Visualization

During this ritual, I replay a vision of my '*ideal day*' in my mind. Not a vague and cloudy image of your day, I mean a clearly thought through movie in your mind. What are you wearing, smelling, seeing, and feeling while you accomplish whatever goal you set out for yourself? I do this for as long as is needed at that moment. If you cannot visualize a goal in your mind, then subconsciously you really don't believe it can happen. You have to literally *see* it to *achieve* it! Go back to the homework assignment where I asked you about your ideal day. Let that tool guide you during this visualization ritual. It will help maintain daily peace and increase your belief in achieving your better and grander life!

Nine: Mirror time

Ok ladies...I know. Most of us are not big on looking at ourselves in the mirror, especially before the make-up and hair are done, for extended periods of time. But even guys tend to never really examine themselves closely. And that's a problem. Your reflection in the mirror is a reflection of God to this world. We need to know what the world is seeing and adjust accordingly if necessary. We also can use this ritual to learn to *love* ourselves as we are! If we cannot speak truth, love, and healing to our own reflection, how in the *world* can we expect those intentions to manifest outside of ourselves? Get close to that mirror and speak *healing*, *love*, *and life* to yourself daily!! This is where your healing, resetting, and rebuilding affirmations will also come into play.

Ten: Imagination

This ritual, while similar to the visualization ritual, is a bit less practically and rationally rooted. This time, you should close your eyes and simply allowing yourself to imagine things you desire to see in your life. Let yourself be unbound by practical concerns or logic. See yourself cliff diving in Bali if that is a dream. Imagine you and your partner making passionate love! Visualize opening your bank account app, checking your investments, and seeing a six figures balance there. Just **dream** for a good ten minutes and watch your atmosphere *shift!*

So, there are your ten options for you to pick from to begin crafting your Daily Intentional Actions. And also realize you can adjust and adapt these as needed depending both on what you're presently experiencing in your life, and your understanding of what will work for you.

Assignment: Create a Peace Toolbox!

1. Select a combination of tools from the above list which work best when you need to re-center and regain your peace! Try them *all* and then decide what connected best with your spirit.

2. Once selected, create a graphic with this list and hang it in your sacred space as a reminder of the power you have to *shift* your energy and atmosphere.

YOU ALWAYS HAVE A CHOICE

EMPOWERMENT - the process of becoming stronger and more confident, especially in controlling one's life and claiming one's rights.

YOU HAVE A *RIGHT* TO A LIFE OF PEACE

Do you know why? You have a right to this experience because of WHO you are: a being created in the image of God designed to experience an abundant life! Take ownership of that! See it as *possible* for yourself now! Please understand this, peace is not an absence of conflict or war (*outside of you*), but a 'sense of completeness, wholeness, and tranquility (*inside of you*) which encourages you to give of yourself generously in life'. When you're living a lifestyle of peace, your default mindset will be one of gratitude and service to others. The need for competition, control, and position will melt away as you settle into a state of **being** grateful, open and receptive to the flow of life.

So, what will you do next?

If you receive anything from reading this book, I need you to take ownership of this simple, yet profound truth: You _**always**_ have a choice! As you journey through this life, you will constantly be faced with situations which demand an answer to this question: Should I _**surrender**_ my peace to others (_i.e. people, situations, circumstances_), or _**maintain**_ my peace to fully embody God's will for my life?

When you give yourself permission to take this journey to greater inner peace, you'll discover the challenges you've faced in the past were all a result of your thinking and beliefs about the situations experienced. There's no one outside of you with enough power to drive you crazy or lose your cool unless you **surrender** that power to them. And many of us do just that because we're unaware of who we truly are and what we truly need to fully experience a prosperous and fulfilling life. And if you think prosperity is only about money, let me share the definition:

> **PROSPERITY** – the condition of being successful or thriving.

True prosperity is when you're 'moving forward and showing progress'. It isn't limited to simply your physical possessions. It extends to the healthy growth and expansion of your inner self as well. As you learn to **understand** your needs, your ability to **shift** your perspective and perception will become sharper and more intentional. From that empowered position, your expanding knowledge of self will become an internal motivator to embody your true self and live your best life. With this elevated vision of your life and purpose, *designing* and maintaining your physical atmosphere will become a welcomed transition from the old to the new! With your renewed mindset and enhanced atmosphere in view, *executing* your Daily Intentional Actions (DIAs) will serve to maintain the flow of love, joy, and peace that will surely be exuding from your life.

Now, I have only one request... *Take Action!* We can talk about the life we want and never live it! We can dream about the life we want and never experience it!

All you have control over is *your actions* right *now*! So, take action! We often look at the larger goals in our life and become daunted by the distance between where we are and where we want to be. Being your best self isn't about where you are at any given moment in your life, it's about directionality. Are you taking steps towards your goals or away from them? Just take that step each day. Do you want to be healthy? Buy a salad rather than a burger today or go for a walk instead of watching television. Do you want to be successful? Connect with one person who is living the life you desire and learn from them or read an autobiography of a person whom you admire! Do *one* thing today that propels you towards your dreams.

You can do this!

Remain in a place of Peace.

No matter what happens today...

Maintain Your *Peace!*

No matter what is said today...

Maintain Your *Peace!*

No matter how you feel today...

Maintain your *Peace* and refuse to

surrender it.

Made in the USA
Middletown, DE
11 January 2019